Introduction

Welcome to the start of finding your way, to the beginning of uncovering your unique self, and processing your thoughts along the way. I am so proud of you for taking these profound steps to look deep within yourself and discover who you are, what you want, and where you want your life to go.

As a Licensed Clinical Social Worker, I've had the honor of assisting many individuals with sorting through their thoughts and feelings and tapping into their true selves. Witnessing my clients reach their moment of self-clarification and unravel their feelings of uncertainty and self-doubt motivates me to continue to uplift and motivate others to do the same.

As you travel through this journal, you will be able to explore your morning and evening reflections, write out your thoughts, and engage in self-discovery. Feel free to use the pages of this journal however your unique journey takes you.

Now with that said, let's gear up, suit up, and take these strides on this exploratory adventure...Your Divine Journey.

Morning Reflections

TODAY I AM FEELING...

_____

_____

_____

_____

TODAY I AM GOING TO...

_____

_____

_____

_____

TODAY I AM LOOKING FORWARD TO...

_____

_____

_____

_____

MY AFFIRMATION TODAY

_____

_____

_____

_____

Evening Reflections

WHAT WENT WELL TODAY?

_____

_____

_____

_____

WHAT CHALLENGES DID I FACE, AND HOW DID I HANDLE THEM?

_____

_____

_____

_____

WHAT EMOTIONS DID I EXPERIENCE TODAY?

_____

_____

_____

_____

WHAT AM I GRATEFUL FOR TODAY?

_____

_____

_____

_____

My Thoughts

Morning Reflections

TODAY I AM FEELING...

_____
_____
_____
_____

TODAY I AM GOING TO...

_____
_____
_____
_____

TODAY I AM LOOKING FORWARD TO...

_____
_____
_____
_____

MY AFFIRMATION TODAY

_____
_____
_____
_____

Evening Reflections

WHAT WENT WELL TODAY?

_____

_____

_____

_____

WHAT CHALLENGES DID I FACE, AND HOW DID I HANDLE THEM?

_____

_____

_____

_____

WHAT EMOTIONS DID I EXPERIENCE TODAY?

_____

_____

_____

_____

WHAT AM I GRATEFUL FOR TODAY?

_____

_____

_____

_____

Ideas & Inspirations

Morning Reflections

TODAY I AM FEELING...

_____

_____

_____

_____

TODAY I AM GOING TO...

_____

_____

_____

_____

TODAY I AM LOOKING FORWARD TO...

_____

_____

_____

_____

MY AFFIRMATION TODAY

_____

_____

_____

_____

Evening Reflections

WHAT WENT WELL TODAY?

_____

_____

_____

_____

WHAT CHALLENGES DID I FACE, AND HOW DID I HANDLE THEM?

_____

_____

_____

_____

WHAT EMOTIONS DID I EXPERIENCE TODAY?

_____

_____

_____

_____

WHAT AM I GRATEFUL FOR TODAY?

_____

_____

_____

_____

OCCUPY
THE
SPACE

CHOOSE A SHAPE AND OCCUPY IT WITH YOUR
THOUGHTS.

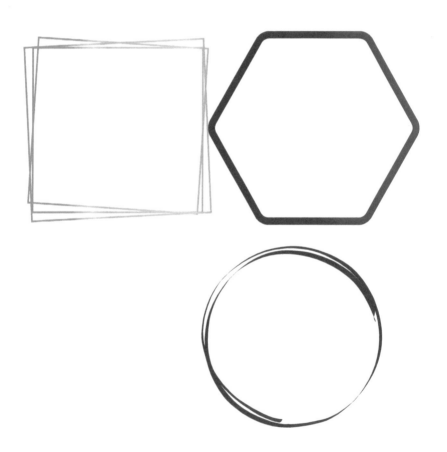

Morning Reflections

TODAY I AM FEELING...

_____

_____

_____

_____

TODAY I AM GOING TO...

_____

_____

_____

_____

TODAY I AM LOOKING FORWARD TO...

_____

_____

_____

_____

MY AFFIRMATION TODAY

_____

_____

_____

_____

Evening Reflections

WHAT WENT WELL TODAY?

_____

_____

_____

_____

WHAT CHALLENGES DID I FACE, AND HOW DID I HANDLE THEM?

_____

_____

_____

_____

WHAT EMOTIONS DID I EXPERIENCE TODAY?

_____

_____

_____

_____

WHAT AM I GRATEFUL FOR TODAY?

_____

_____

_____

_____

Own Your Journey

WHAT DOES OWNING YOUR JOURNEY LOOK LIKE?

Morning Reflections

TODAY I AM FEELING...

_____

_____

_____

_____

TODAY I AM GOING TO...

_____

_____

_____

_____

TODAY I AM LOOKING FORWARD TO...

_____

_____

_____

_____

MY AFFIRMATION TODAY

_____

_____

_____

_____

Evening Reflections

WHAT WENT WELL TODAY?

_____
_____
_____
_____

WHAT CHALLENGES DID I FACE, AND HOW DID I HANDLE THEM?

_____
_____
_____
_____

WHAT EMOTIONS DID I EXPERIENCE TODAY?

_____
_____
_____
_____

WHAT AM I GRATEFUL FOR TODAY?

_____
_____
_____
_____

LOVE
yourself

be
happy ♡

MANIFESTING

SELF
LOVE

Dream
Big

you
are
loved

Never
TOO
Late

be
Brave

Morning Reflections

TODAY I AM FEELING...

_____
_____
_____
_____

TODAY I AM GOING TO...

_____
_____
_____
_____

TODAY I AM LOOKING FORWARD TO...

_____
_____
_____
_____

MY AFFIRMATION TODAY

_____
_____
_____
_____

Evening Reflections

WHAT WENT WELL TODAY?

_____

_____

_____

_____

WHAT CHALLENGES DID I FACE, AND HOW DID I HANDLE THEM?

_____

_____

_____

_____

WHAT EMOTIONS DID I EXPERIENCE TODAY?

_____

_____

_____

_____

WHAT AM I GRATEFUL FOR TODAY?

_____

_____

_____

_____

Self-Care Tips

- PRIORITIZE SLEEP
- PRACTICE MINDFULNESS
- NOURISH YOUR BODY
- MOVE YOUR BODY
- SET BOUNDARIES
- UNPLUG AND DISCONNECT
- PRACTICE GRATITUDE
- TAKE TIME FOR YOURSELF
- PRACTICE DEEP BREATHING
- LISTEN TO YOUR BODY
- ENGAGE IN POSITIVE SELF-TALK
- SPEND TIME IN NATURE
- PAMPER YOURSELF
- SEEK SUPPORT WHEN NEEDED

Morning Reflections

TODAY I AM FEELING...

_____

_____

_____

_____

TODAY I AM GOING TO...

_____

_____

_____

_____

TODAY I AM LOOKING FORWARD TO...

_____

_____

_____

_____

MY AFFIRMATION TODAY

_____

_____

_____

_____

Evening Reflections

WHAT WENT WELL TODAY?

_____

_____

_____

_____

WHAT CHALLENGES DID I FACE, AND HOW DID I HANDLE THEM?

_____

_____

_____

_____

WHAT EMOTIONS DID I EXPERIENCE TODAY?

_____

_____

_____

_____

WHAT AM I GRATEFUL FOR TODAY?

_____

_____

_____

_____

Morning Reflections

TODAY I AM FEELING...

_____
_____
_____
_____

TODAY I AM GOING TO...

_____
_____
_____
_____

TODAY I AM LOOKING FORWARD TO...

_____
_____
_____
_____

MY AFFIRMATION TODAY

_____
_____
_____
_____

Evening Reflections

WHAT WENT WELL TODAY?

_____
_____
_____
_____

WHAT CHALLENGES DID I FACE, AND HOW DID I HANDLE THEM?

_____
_____
_____
_____

WHAT EMOTIONS DID I EXPERIENCE TODAY?

_____
_____
_____
_____

WHAT AM I GRATEFUL FOR TODAY?

_____
_____
_____
_____

YOU ARE CAPABLE

of...

- DOING GREAT THINGS
- ACHIEVING GOALS
- MAKING WISE DECISIONS
- CHOOSING YOU

Morning Reflections

TODAY I AM FEELING...

_____

_____

_____

_____

TODAY I AM GOING TO...

_____

_____

_____

_____

TODAY I AM LOOKING FORWARD TO...

_____

_____

_____

_____

MY AFFIRMATION TODAY

_____

_____

_____

_____

Evening Reflections

WHAT WENT WELL TODAY?

_____

_____

_____

_____

WHAT CHALLENGES DID I FACE, AND HOW DID I HANDLE THEM?

_____

_____

_____

_____

WHAT EMOTIONS DID I EXPERIENCE TODAY?

_____

_____

_____

_____

WHAT AM I GRATEFUL FOR TODAY?

_____

_____

_____

_____

Morning Reflections

TODAY I AM FEELING...

_____

_____

_____

_____

TODAY I AM GOING TO...

_____

_____

_____

_____

TODAY I AM LOOKING FORWARD TO...

_____

_____

_____

_____

MY AFFIRMATION TODAY

_____

_____

_____

_____

Evening Reflections

WHAT WENT WELL TODAY?

_____

_____

_____

_____

WHAT CHALLENGES DID I FACE, AND HOW DID I HANDLE THEM?

_____

_____

_____

_____

WHAT EMOTIONS DID I EXPERIENCE TODAY?

_____

_____

_____

_____

WHAT AM I GRATEFUL FOR TODAY?

_____

_____

_____

_____

YOU ARE DOING GREAT!

Morning Reflections

TODAY I AM FEELING...

_____
_____
_____
_____

TODAY I AM GOING TO...

_____
_____
_____
_____

TODAY I AM LOOKING FORWARD TO...

_____
_____
_____
_____

MY AFFIRMATION TODAY

_____
_____
_____
_____

Evening Reflections

WHAT WENT WELL TODAY?

_____

_____

_____

_____

WHAT CHALLENGES DID I FACE, AND HOW DID I HANDLE THEM?

_____

_____

_____

_____

WHAT EMOTIONS DID I EXPERIENCE TODAY?

_____

_____

_____

_____

WHAT AM I GRATEFUL FOR TODAY?

_____

_____

_____

_____

Positive Affirmations

I AM WORTHY OF LOVE, HAPPINESS, & SUCCESS.

I TRUST IN MY ABILITY TO OVERCOME CHALLENGES.

I AM ENOUGH JUST AS I AM.

I AM IN CONTROL OF MY THOUGHTS, FEELINGS, AND ACTIONS.

I CHOOSE TO FOCUS ON THE POSITIVE ASPECTS OF MY LIFE.

I EMBRACE CHANGE AND WELCOME NEW OPPORTUNITIES.

I AM CONFIDENT IN MY ABILITIES AND TRUST MY DECISIONS.

I AM DESERVING OF ALL THE GOOD THINGS THAT COME MY WAY.

Morning Reflections

TODAY I AM FEELING...

_____

_____

_____

_____

TODAY I AM GOING TO...

_____

_____

_____

_____

TODAY I AM LOOKING FORWARD TO...

_____

_____

_____

_____

MY AFFIRMATION TODAY

_____

_____

_____

Evening Reflections

WHAT WENT WELL TODAY?

_____

_____

_____

_____

WHAT CHALLENGES DID I FACE, AND HOW DID I HANDLE THEM?

_____

_____

_____

_____

WHAT EMOTIONS DID I EXPERIENCE TODAY?

_____

_____

_____

_____

WHAT AM I GRATEFUL FOR TODAY?

_____

_____

_____

_____

Things that make
you smile

Morning Reflections

TODAY I AM FEELING...

_____

_____

_____

_____

TODAY I AM GOING TO...

_____

_____

_____

_____

TODAY I AM LOOKING FORWARD TO...

_____

_____

_____

_____

MY AFFIRMATION TODAY

_____

_____

_____

_____

Evening Reflections

WHAT WENT WELL TODAY?

_____

_____

_____

_____

WHAT CHALLENGES DID I FACE, AND HOW DID I HANDLE THEM?

_____

_____

_____

_____

WHAT EMOTIONS DID I EXPERIENCE TODAY?

_____

_____

_____

_____

WHAT AM I GRATEFUL FOR TODAY?

_____

_____

_____

_____

Stop worrying about things you can't control

Morning Reflections

TODAY I AM FEELING...

_____

_____

_____

_____

TODAY I AM GOING TO...

_____

_____

_____

_____

TODAY I AM LOOKING FORWARD TO...

_____

_____

_____

_____

MY AFFIRMATION TODAY

_____

_____

_____

_____

Evening Reflections

WHAT WENT WELL TODAY?

_____

_____

_____

_____

WHAT CHALLENGES DID I FACE, AND HOW DID I HANDLE THEM?

_____

_____

_____

_____

WHAT EMOTIONS DID I EXPERIENCE TODAY?

_____

_____

_____

_____

WHAT AM I GRATEFUL FOR TODAY?

_____

_____

_____

_____

grow through
what you go
through

Morning Reflections

TODAY I AM FEELING...

_____

_____

_____

_____

TODAY I AM GOING TO...

_____

_____

_____

_____

TODAY I AM LOOKING FORWARD TO...

_____

_____

_____

_____

MY AFFIRMATION TODAY

_____

_____

_____

_____

Evening Reflections

WHAT WENT WELL TODAY?

_____

_____

_____

_____

WHAT CHALLENGES DID I FACE, AND HOW DID I HANDLE THEM?

_____

_____

_____

_____

WHAT EMOTIONS DID I EXPERIENCE TODAY?

_____

_____

_____

_____

WHAT AM I GRATEFUL FOR TODAY?

_____

_____

_____

_____

Believe

Morning Reflections

TODAY I AM FEELING...

_____
_____
_____
_____

TODAY I AM GOING TO...

_____
_____
_____
_____

TODAY I AM LOOKING FORWARD TO...

_____
_____
_____
_____

MY AFFIRMATION TODAY

_____
_____
_____
_____

Evening Reflections

WHAT WENT WELL TODAY?

_____

_____

_____

_____

WHAT CHALLENGES DID I FACE, AND HOW DID I HANDLE THEM?

_____

_____

_____

_____

WHAT EMOTIONS DID I EXPERIENCE TODAY?

_____

_____

_____

_____

WHAT AM I GRATEFUL FOR TODAY?

_____

_____

_____

_____

WHAT BRINGS YOU JOY?

_____
_____
_____
_____
_____
_____
_____
_____
_____
_____
_____
_____
_____
_____
_____
_____
_____
_____
_____
_____
_____
_____
_____
_____
_____
_____
_____
_____

Morning Reflections

TODAY I AM FEELING...

_____

_____

_____

_____

TODAY I AM GOING TO...

_____

_____

_____

_____

TODAY I AM LOOKING FORWARD TO...

_____

_____

_____

_____

MY AFFIRMATION TODAY

_____

_____

_____

_____

Evening Reflections

WHAT WENT WELL TODAY?

_____

_____

_____

_____

WHAT CHALLENGES DID I FACE, AND HOW DID I HANDLE THEM?

_____

_____

_____

_____

WHAT EMOTIONS DID I EXPERIENCE TODAY?

_____

_____

_____

_____

WHAT AM I GRATEFUL FOR TODAY?

_____

_____

_____

_____

Morning Reflections

TODAY I AM FEELING...

_____

_____

_____

_____

TODAY I AM GOING TO...

_____

_____

_____

_____

TODAY I AM LOOKING FORWARD TO...

_____

_____

_____

_____

MY AFFIRMATION TODAY

_____

_____

_____

_____

Evening Reflections

WHAT WENT WELL TODAY?

_____

_____

_____

_____

WHAT CHALLENGES DID I FACE, AND HOW DID I HANDLE THEM?

_____

_____

_____

_____

WHAT EMOTIONS DID I EXPERIENCE TODAY?

_____

_____

_____

_____

WHAT AM I GRATEFUL FOR TODAY?

_____

_____

_____

_____

Morning Reflections

TODAY I AM FEELING...

_____

_____

_____

_____

TODAY I AM GOING TO...

_____

_____

_____

_____

TODAY I AM LOOKING FORWARD TO...

_____

_____

_____

_____

MY AFFIRMATION TODAY

_____

_____

_____

_____

Evening Reflections

WHAT WENT WELL TODAY?

_____

_____

_____

_____

WHAT CHALLENGES DID I FACE, AND HOW DID I HANDLE THEM?

_____

_____

_____

_____

WHAT EMOTIONS DID I EXPERIENCE TODAY?

_____

_____

_____

_____

WHAT AM I GRATEFUL FOR TODAY?

_____

_____

_____

_____

Morning Reflections

TODAY I AM FEELING...

_____
_____
_____
_____

TODAY I AM GOING TO...

_____
_____
_____
_____

TODAY I AM LOOKING FORWARD TO...

_____
_____
_____
_____

MY AFFIRMATION TODAY

_____
_____
_____
_____

Evening Reflections

WHAT WENT WELL TODAY?

_____

_____

_____

_____

WHAT CHALLENGES DID I FACE, AND HOW DID I HANDLE THEM?

_____

_____

_____

_____

WHAT EMOTIONS DID I EXPERIENCE TODAY?

_____

_____

_____

_____

WHAT AM I GRATEFUL FOR TODAY?

_____

_____

_____

_____

HOW ARE YOU STRONGER TODAY THAN YOU WERE YESTERDAY?

Morning Reflections

TODAY I AM FEELING...

_____

_____

_____

_____

TODAY I AM GOING TO...

_____

_____

_____

_____

TODAY I AM LOOKING FORWARD TO...

_____

_____

_____

_____

MY AFFIRMATION TODAY

_____

_____

_____

_____

Evening Reflections

WHAT WENT WELL TODAY?

_____

_____

_____

_____

WHAT CHALLENGES DID I FACE, AND HOW DID I HANDLE THEM?

_____

_____

_____

_____

WHAT EMOTIONS DID I EXPERIENCE TODAY?

_____

_____

_____

_____

WHAT AM I GRATEFUL FOR TODAY?

_____

_____

_____

_____

GRATITUDE

Morning Reflections

TODAY I AM FEELING...

_____

_____

_____

_____

TODAY I AM GOING TO...

_____

_____

_____

_____

TODAY I AM LOOKING FORWARD TO...

_____

_____

_____

_____

MY AFFIRMATION TODAY

_____

_____

_____

_____

Evening Reflections

WHAT WENT WELL TODAY?

_____

_____

_____

_____

WHAT CHALLENGES DID I FACE, AND HOW DID I HANDLE THEM?

_____

_____

_____

_____

WHAT EMOTIONS DID I EXPERIENCE TODAY?

_____

_____

_____

_____

WHAT AM I GRATEFUL FOR TODAY?

_____

_____

_____

_____

Adventure awaits

Morning Reflections

TODAY I AM FEELING...

_____

_____

_____

_____

TODAY I AM GOING TO...

_____

_____

_____

_____

TODAY I AM LOOKING FORWARD TO...

_____

_____

_____

_____

MY AFFIRMATION TODAY

_____

_____

_____

_____

Evening Reflections

WHAT WENT WELL TODAY?

_____

_____

_____

_____

WHAT CHALLENGES DID I FACE, AND HOW DID I HANDLE THEM?

_____

_____

_____

_____

WHAT EMOTIONS DID I EXPERIENCE TODAY?

_____

_____

_____

_____

WHAT AM I GRATEFUL FOR TODAY?

_____

_____

_____

_____

Be Kind.

Be Happy

Be HUMBLE

be thankful

be you

Morning Reflections

TODAY I AM FEELING...

_____

_____

_____

_____

TODAY I AM GOING TO...

_____

_____

_____

_____

TODAY I AM LOOKING FORWARD TO...

_____

_____

_____

_____

MY AFFIRMATION TODAY

_____

_____

_____

_____

Evening Reflections

WHAT WENT WELL TODAY?

_____

_____

_____

_____

WHAT CHALLENGES DID I FACE, AND HOW DID I HANDLE THEM?

_____

_____

_____

_____

WHAT EMOTIONS DID I EXPERIENCE TODAY?

_____

_____

_____

_____

WHAT AM I GRATEFUL FOR TODAY?

_____

_____

_____

_____

THIS IS YOUR SPACE TO BE YOU! DRAW, DOODLE, SCRIBBLE...

Morning Reflections

TODAY I AM FEELING...

_____

_____

_____

_____

TODAY I AM GOING TO...

_____

_____

_____

_____

TODAY I AM LOOKING FORWARD TO...

_____

_____

_____

_____

MY AFFIRMATION TODAY

_____

_____

_____

_____

Evening Reflections

WHAT WENT WELL TODAY?

_____

_____

_____

_____

WHAT CHALLENGES DID I FACE, AND HOW DID I HANDLE THEM?

_____

_____

_____

_____

WHAT EMOTIONS DID I EXPERIENCE TODAY?

_____

_____

_____

WHAT AM I GRATEFUL FOR TODAY?

_____

_____

_____

Morning Reflections

TODAY I AM FEELING...

_____

_____

_____

_____

TODAY I AM GOING TO...

_____

_____

_____

_____

TODAY I AM LOOKING FORWARD TO...

_____

_____

_____

_____

MY AFFIRMATION TODAY

_____

_____

_____

_____

Evening Reflections

WHAT WENT WELL TODAY?

_____
_____
_____
_____

WHAT CHALLENGES DID I FACE, AND HOW DID I HANDLE THEM?

_____
_____
_____
_____

WHAT EMOTIONS DID I EXPERIENCE TODAY?

_____
_____
_____
_____

WHAT AM I GRATEFUL FOR TODAY?

_____
_____
_____
_____

trust your
JOURNEY

Morning Reflections

TODAY I AM FEELING...

_____

_____

_____

_____

TODAY I AM GOING TO...

_____

_____

_____

_____

TODAY I AM LOOKING FORWARD TO...

_____

_____

_____

_____

MY AFFIRMATION TODAY

_____

_____

_____

_____

Evening Reflections

WHAT WENT WELL TODAY?

_____

_____

_____

_____

WHAT CHALLENGES DID I FACE, AND HOW DID I HANDLE THEM?

_____

_____

_____

_____

WHAT EMOTIONS DID I EXPERIENCE TODAY?

_____

_____

_____

WHAT AM I GRATEFUL FOR TODAY?

_____

_____

_____

_____

LIFE IS TOUGH
But So
Are You

Morning Reflections

TODAY I AM FEELING...

_____
_____
_____
_____

TODAY I AM GOING TO...

_____
_____
_____
_____

TODAY I AM LOOKING FORWARD TO...

_____
_____
_____
_____

MY AFFIRMATION TODAY

_____
_____
_____
_____

Evening Reflections

WHAT WENT WELL TODAY?

_____
_____
_____
_____

WHAT CHALLENGES DID I FACE, AND HOW DID I HANDLE THEM?

_____
_____
_____
_____

WHAT EMOTIONS DID I EXPERIENCE TODAY?

_____
_____
_____
_____

WHAT AM I GRATEFUL FOR TODAY?

_____
_____
_____
_____

Thoughts
have energy.
Make sure
your thoughts
are positive &
powerful.

Morning Reflections

TODAY I AM FEELING...

_____
_____
_____
_____

TODAY I AM GOING TO...

_____
_____
_____
_____

TODAY I AM LOOKING FORWARD TO...

_____
_____
_____
_____

MY AFFIRMATION TODAY

_____
_____
_____

Evening Reflections

WHAT WENT WELL TODAY?

_____

_____

_____

_____

WHAT CHALLENGES DID I FACE, AND HOW DID I HANDLE THEM?

_____

_____

_____

_____

WHAT EMOTIONS DID I EXPERIENCE TODAY?

_____

_____

_____

_____

WHAT AM I GRATEFUL FOR TODAY?

_____

_____

_____

_____

EVERYTHING YOU NEED IS ALREADY INSIDE

Morning Reflections

TODAY I AM FEELING...

_____

_____

_____

_____

TODAY I AM GOING TO...

_____

_____

_____

_____

TODAY I AM LOOKING FORWARD TO...

_____

_____

_____

_____

MY AFFIRMATION TODAY

_____

_____

_____

_____

Evening Reflections

WHAT WENT WELL TODAY?

_____

_____

_____

_____

WHAT CHALLENGES DID I FACE, AND HOW DID I HANDLE THEM?

_____

_____

_____

_____

WHAT EMOTIONS DID I EXPERIENCE TODAY?

_____

_____

_____

_____

WHAT AM I GRATEFUL FOR TODAY?

_____

_____

_____

_____

My Thoughts

My Thoughts

My Thoughts

My Thoughts

My Thoughts

My Thoughts

My Thoughts

My Thoughts

As you reach the end of this journal, take a moment to honor the progress you've made. Each entry reflects your commitment to self-discovery, growth, and healing. The journey of self-care is ongoing, and every step, no matter how small, brings you closer to understanding yourself more deeply. Remember that growth isn't always linear, but persistence is key. Trust in your strength, continue to show up for yourself, and know that the more you invest in your well-being, the more resilient and empowered you become. Keep going- you're worth the effort.

find your own Path

Your Divine Journey, LLC
www.yourdivinejourneyllc.com

Made in United States
Troutdale, OR
12/11/2024